£4.99

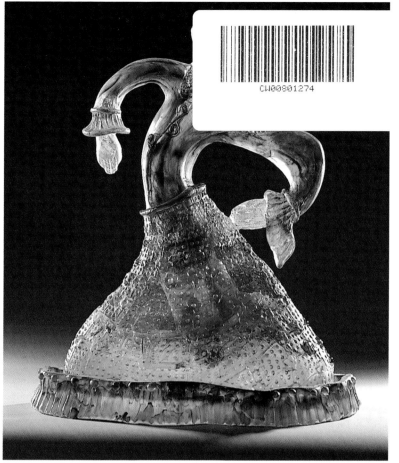

'Dancing King' by Tlws Johnson, late 1990s. Kiln-cast using recycled glass from Dartington Crystal.

Studio Glass
1960–2000
Graham McLaren

A Shire book

Published in 2002 by Shire Publications Ltd,
Cromwell House, Church Street, Princes Risborough,
Buckinghamshire HP27 9AA, UK.
(Website: www.shirebooks.co.uk)

Copyright © 2002 by Graham McLaren.
First published 2002.
Shire Album 403. ISBN 0 7478 0527 X.
Graham McLaren is hereby identified as the author of this
work in accordance with Section 77 of the Copyright,
Designs and Patents Act 1988.

British Library Cataloguing in Publication Data:
McLaren, Graham
Studio glass, 1960–2000. (A shire book)
1. Art glass – Great Britain – History –20th century
2. Glass artists – Great Britain
I. Title
748.2'941'09045
ISBN 0 7478 0527 X

Front cover: *'Bird Bottles' by Catherine Hough.*
Back cover: *'Double Cased Whale Plate', 1992, by Malcolm Sutcliffe.*

ACKNOWLEDGEMENTS

I thank all the makers who have so generously supplied information and illustrations for this book. In particular, my gratitude goes to Brian and Jenny Blanthorn, John Cook, Diana Hobson, Shital Pattani, Professor Ronald Pennell, David Reekie, Colin Reid, Pauline Solven and Anthony Stern.

Photographs are acknowledged as follows: Paula Andrews, page 17 (bottom); Rick Beattie, page 16 (bottom); Jane Beebe, page 34 (centre); Brian and Jenny Blanthorn, page 36 (bottom two); Blowzone, page 5 (bottom); Amanda Brisbane, page 18 (bottom); Broadfield House Glass Museum/David Reekie, page 39 (left); Norman Stuart Clarke, pages 15 (top; bottom), 43 (both); Katharine Coleman, page 26 (bottom left); Ros Conway, page 21 (centre); John H. Cook, pages 19 (left), 30 (top); Corning Museum of Glass, Corning, New York, pages 27 (bottom), 29 (bottom); George Coupe, page 38 (top); Gillian Mannings Cox, page 16 (top two); Crafts Council, page 42 (centre); Crafts Council/Ian Dobbie, page 34 (top left); Dartington Crystal Ltd, pages 5 (top), 8 (top; bottom left); Sue Dawes, page 6 (all); Peter Dreiser, pages 26 (bottom right), 27 (top); E & M Glass, page 4 (bottom); David Fisher, page 1; Deborah Fladgate, pages 25 (both), 33 (top); Peter Freeman, page 24 (top right); Hugh Gilbert, page 3; Morag Gordon, page 37 (bottom); Cliff Guttridge, page 44 (all); Sam Herman, pages 11 (top), 29 (right); Maggie Hilton, page 20 (bottom two); Diana Hobson, pages 21 (bottom left), 31 (bottom right), 32 (top); Peter Hodsoll, pages 17 (centre), 32 (bottom); Catherine Hough, front cover; Fiona Houghton-Parker, pages 22 (lower two), 26 (top two); Sean Hunter, page 23 (both); Keith James, page 22 (top); Tlws Johnson, page 21 (top); Dave Jones, pages 35 (centre; bottom), 36 (top); Journeaux, www.journeaux.org, page 37 (top; centre); Richard Kalina, page 32 (centre); June Kingsbury, pages 15 (centre), 17 (top); Dan Klein collection/David Reekie, page 39 (top right); Peter Layton, pages 46, 47; Liz Lowe, page 18 (top); William Manson Snr, page 24 (top left; bottom); Neil McCutcheon, page 22 (upper centre); Kerry Morgan, page 9 (top); National Glass Centre, Sunderland, pages 13 (bottom), 45 (bottom); Ronald Pennell, page 39 (bottom); David Reekie, pages 20 (top three), 38 (bottom); Colin Reid, page 37 (bottom two); Guus Rijven, page 33 (bottom); Bruno Romanelli, page 45 (top right); Karlin Rushbrooke, page 40 (top); Ken Smith, page 45 (top); Pauline Solven, pages 14 (all), 30 (bottom), 31 (top two); Anthony Stern, page 7 (top); Malcolm Sutcliffe, page 4 (top), back cover; David Taylor, page 42 (bottom); Louis Thompson, page 13 (top); Angela Thwaites, page 35 (top); Fleur Tookey, pages 40 (bottom), 41 (top two); Victoria and Albert Museum, page 31 (bottom left); Victoria and Albert Museum/Ros Conway, page 21 (bottom right); Victoria and Albert Museum/Ken Smith, page 45 (centre).

Printed in Malta by Gutenberg Press Limited, Gudja Road, Tarxien PLA 19, Malta.

Contents

A panoramic view of the interior of Anthony Stern's workshop, 2001.

'Elephant Bowl' by Malcolm Sutcliffe, 2001.

Introduction

Studio glass is among the liveliest areas of the decorative arts to have emerged in Britain during the second half of the twentieth century. It has taken a bright, bold and imaginative approach to an ancient material.

Mankind has made glass for over four thousand years, but the material has never been easy to create or manipulate. Achieving and maintaining the temperatures sufficient to produce molten glass is difficult. Fuel costs and the sophisticated technologies required meant that until the Second World War glass-making in Britain usually took place only in the factory. Technological progress after the war saw advances in both heating methods and the materials used for glass. These developments, together with a supportive educational and artistic atmosphere, allowed glass-making to develop as a studio activity for individuals and small groups.

Examples of hand-blown glass from the 'Flim Flam' range of E & M Glass, Cheshire, 2000.

Swedish glass-blowers working at the Dartington factory, 1967.

Studio Glass 1960–2000 will show how this has resulted in an exciting and dynamic range of approaches to glass. It will examine how the early years of studio glass in Britain were dominated by 'hot' methods of making, primarily concerning the blown form. Innovation and invention marked the 1980s and 1990s, in which the boundaries of glass-making technology applied to individual making activity have been extended. The outcome of this is a movement that recognises the legitimacy of a wide range of glass-making activity.

British studio glass-making is truly international in its outlook, drawing inspiration from the work of makers in America, Europe and elsewhere. Detailed consideration of foreign work is outside the scope of this book, however. The aim is to introduce the reader to this lively area of British crafts, giving an overview of the variety of glass objects produced and the processes behind their production.

Figurative glass range by 'Blowzone', the partnership of Iestyn and Beverley Davies, late 1990s.

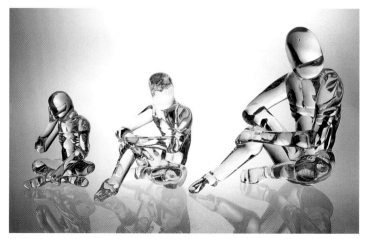

Mosaic glass by Sue Dawes, made by a process that was first developed during the Roman period and involves fusing together pre-formed glass tesserae.

A rich past

It is important to recognise that the history and traditions of glass-making have played a central role in the development of studio glass. The earliest known glass objects are beads made in Mesopotamia *c*.2500 BC. They are probably the products of family groups of craftspeople. These tiny objects indicate a struggle to achieve adequate temperatures for glass-making. The development of furnace technology seems to have been fairly slow.

The Roman period saw the greatest development in glass-making. Its innovations still form the largest body of skills and techniques used by studio glass-makers. They include glass-blowing, developed by Syrian glass-makers *c*.50 BC. Two basic approaches to the process, blowing into a mould and 'free' blowing, were quickly developed to produce a huge range of forms.

A detail of one of the glass tesserae that make up Sue Dawes's mosaic pieces.

Sue Dawes drawing out the glass rod that will be cut up to form the tesserae for her mosaic pieces.

The Portland Vase (AD c.50) represents paramount blowing skill and a masterly understanding of the chemistry of glass-making. To the Victorians the Portland Vase epitomised the grace and artistry of classical antiquity. The method of its making, combining 'hot' and 'cold' techniques with cut decoration, echoed the lead-glass tradition that dominated British glass-making from the late seventeenth century. Lead glass is based on the addition of lead oxide to the glass composition (also containing silica and lime), allowing the glass to melt at a lower temperature. Lead 'crystal' (the popular name for lead glass) has clarity and refractivity, making it particularly suitable for cut decoration.

Above: 'Honeycomb Vase' by Anthony Stern, mid 1990s. Blowing the glass into a metal cage, Stern is paying homage to a glass-making process first developed by Roman glass-makers.

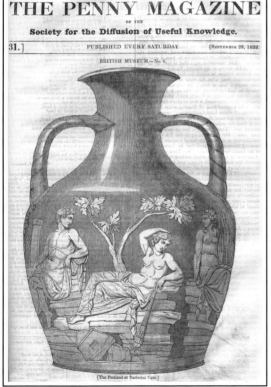

The front cover of *The Penny Magazine*, September 1832. By the Victorian period the Portland Vase was an object of popular veneration, symbolising classical grace and skill.

Dartington Crystal Ltd has been making lead crystal by hand at Torrington, Devon, since 1967. It is a key interface between industrial and studio glass-making and gives generous support to glass education through annual competitions and prizes for student work.

Above: The Stourbridge glass engraver at work, from Apsley Pellatt's *Curiosities of Glassmaking* (London, 1849).

Left: 'Sharon' by Frank Thrower for Dartington Crystal (1971) is a modern interpretation of the English lead-crystal tradition. It was exhibited at the Victoria and Albert Museum as one of the hundred best ever British designs, alongside Concorde and the Mini! It is still being produced.

Andrew Potter's 'Façon de Venise' pieces are a modern interpretation of traditional Venetian forms. Left to right: Reticello wine glass, Reticello Comport dish, Rigadin wine glass.

The development of lead crystal signalled a rejection of the soda glass used by the glass-makers of Renaissance Venice. Soda glass had been refined to produce Cristallo, a glass of exceptional clarity and ductility. The Venetians learned much of the chemistry of colouring glass from Syrian glass-makers, who had perfected techniques of glass colouring and enamelling. Cristallo was excellently suited for hot work where decoration was applied while the glass was still in a plastic state.

By the late nineteenth century, these two traditions of soda and lead glass-making were at the centre of a philosophical debate in Britain. Reformers of the Arts and Crafts Movement saw the division of labour inherent within cut glass as anathema, epitomised by the

The frontispiece to Thomas Bolas's *Glass Blowing and Working* (London, 1898) recommended these Venetian-inspired shapes as appropriate forms for the amateur glass-maker to copy.

9

Glass vases by Powell & Sons (Whitefriars Glass) *c*.1898. These copies of Venetian originals reflect the company's adherence to the principles of the Arts and Crafts Movement.

art critic John Ruskin, who argued that '… all cut glass is barbarous, for the cutting conceals its ductility and confuses it with crystal. Also, all very neat, finished, and perfect form in glass is barbarous.' To Ruskin the soda tradition, emphasising the immediacy of decoration and the skill of the craftsperson, was an antidote to the clinical perfection of cutting.

French glass-makers, including Emile Gallé and Henri Cros, furthered the art of glass-making on both a technical and a philosophical level. They looked to the ideas of the British Arts and Crafts Movement and the writings of critics such as Viollet le Duc,

A Stourbridge industrial glasshouse at work, from Apsley Pellatt's *Curiosities of Glassmaking* (London, 1849).

10

extolling the creative virtues of the 'fortuitous accident' that made each piece of handmade glass unique.

These pioneers represent a bridge between the factory and the studio. They utilised a wide range of (usually rediscovered) techniques from their own experiments and from the work of nineteenth-century industry. In the way that they approached the material, they were less innovative. Gallé, for instance, was the beneficiary of a substantial family fortune. He was able to employ skilled craftspeople to do the day-to-day glass-making for him. He made little of the glass himself.

This changed with the work of the French glass-maker Maurice Marinot. Originally part of the Fauvist painting circle, he had experimented in glass decoration before the First World War. By the 1930s he was working alone, except for the aid of a single assistant, and grappling with the complexities of hot-glass working with remarkable results. In his attitude to 'contact' with the material, he links pre- and post-Second-World-War thinking.

'Form 1' by Sam Herman in free-blown coloured glass.

The role of American innovators, particularly Harvey Littleton and Dominick Labino, must be acknowledged. They were key catalysts to the development of studio glass during the late 1950s and the 1960s. Working with others, Littleton and Labino created a movement centring on glass-blowing. Littleton was perfectly positioned for this. A successful studio potter, he had been brought up in a glass-making family. Littleton caught the tide of change sweeping from the avant-garde art schools of West Coast America. First seen in ceramics, the new crafts philosophy drew from the ideas of Abstract Expressionism, particularly the concern with action and the significance of the moment of creation.

Littleton quickly recognised the significance of these ideas. In his search for a way to 'return glass to the individual artist, to develop a technology for working alone', Littleton worked with the great glass technologist Dominick Labino. They developed a small-scale furnace suitable for teaching on and demonstrating with. Labino had already developed an economical glass that was able to melt at low temperatures and was suitable for their new furnace.

Demonstrations that they gave, together with their continuing development of the technology, led by 1963 to a new hot-glass course at the University of Wisconsin. This was the first of many established in the United States and abroad during the 1960s and 1970s.

A female student at the Royal College of Art, 1963, has her design made up by the resident glass-maker, Mr W. Heaton.

Student work at the Stourbridge College of Art, 1963.

An early graduate was Sam Herman, who brought the new ideas to Britain. His philosophy followed Littleton's belief that 'a blistered, mottled, collapsed, unidentifiable handblown glass object may be more valuable than a crystal swan'. This way of thinking was unlike that encouraged by the glass courses already available in Britain, where the emphasis was strongly on vocational education for industry. Students rarely had access to hot glass, being expected instead to produce drawings that would be made up by glass craftsmen.

The new ideology suited the shift in art schools and (later) the new polytechnics away from the purely vocational. After a period at the Edinburgh College of Art, Herman was invited to start the first British hot-glass course at the Royal College of Art in London in 1967. This was followed by the initiation of several similar courses around Britain during the late 1960s and the 1970s.

A free-blown vase with colour inclusions by Sam Herman, sold at The Glasshouse, London, in 1970.

12

Technology and creativity

Blown glass

The technique of blowing used by studio glass-makers is one that has been used and refined in glass-making for many hundreds of years. As well as the steel blowing iron known as the 'punty', a key tool for the glass-blower is the 'chair'. This refers to the wooden workbench at which the glass-maker sits during making. Only a few other tools are essential. These include the marver, a steel slab that helps to shape the molten glass on the end of the blowing iron, various types of tongs or 'pucellas' used for further manipulation, and the 'block', which can be either a cup-shaped wooden mould or, more commonly nowadays, a thick pad of wet newspaper.

Blowing involves deft manipulation and timing. The glass-maker has to read the temperature and ductility of the glass by its colour, a rose-red glow being an ideal

Above: 'Screaming Head at Pilchuck' by Louis Thompson, 1999. An example of free-blown glass at its most exuberant.

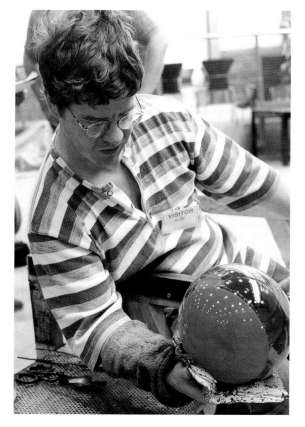

Ed Burke using a wet newspaper 'block' to help shape the hot glass during a demonstration at the National Glass Centre, Sunderland, in 1999.

Pauline Solven blowing at her first studio, in Ravenshill, in 1975. A 'tank style' glass furnace is behind.

working temperature. The glass is frequently reheated during making. Care is taken to overcome forces of gravity that can make the glass drip or fall off the end of the pipe.

These difficulties make free blowing a challenging approach for those working on their own. Perhaps as a result, many graduates of the pioneering glass courses moved away from expressing themselves solely through free blowing and adopted other techniques.

Variations on the basic blowing technique include the addition of hot (plastic) coloured glass at various stages of blowing. The colouring of glass using metallic oxides was known to the earliest glass-makers. Iron oxide can be added to produce a range of colours from yellows and greens through to an almost opaque black. Copper can be used to create blue-toned glass.

Below left: Pauline Solven is one of very few studio makers to practise glass-blowing on her own. Here she is working solo in Sweden (1969) to produce a goblet.

Below right: 'Winged Scent Bottle' by Pauline Solven, 1976.

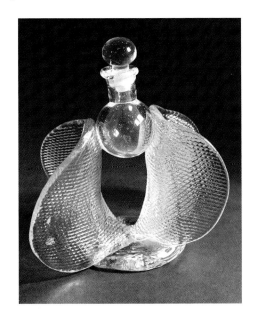

Norman Stuart Clarke applying hot glass to the vessel form, London, 1982.

Below: 'Beached' by Samantha Sweet, 1999. This blown glass has an inner casing of blue and has been cut, masked, sandblasted and polished. It has nylon attachments.

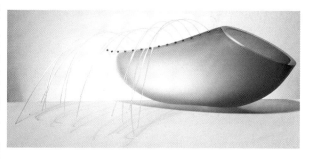

Studio glass-makers use colours that are usually bought 'off the shelf' from specialist manufacturers. Melting entire batches of colour is expensive and wasteful. Techniques such as casing are used instead. In this process, a small blob, or 'gob', of coloured glass is melted and then 'cased' with a clear layer. Re-heating and then blowing the combination results in the colour forming a thin internal layer, effectively fooling the eye into believing that the entire piece is made of coloured glass.

Variations of colouring techniques include marvering, or rolling, fragments of glass into the hot surface. When larger pieces of glass

Norman Stuart Clarke marvering the hot glass, London, 1982.

15

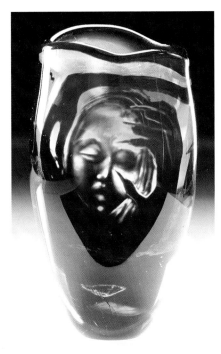

Above left: A Graal 'embryo' by Gillian Mannings Cox, which, after working, is re-heated, blown and cased in clear glass.

Above right: 'Bride', made by Gillian Mannings Cox using the Graal technique, 2000.

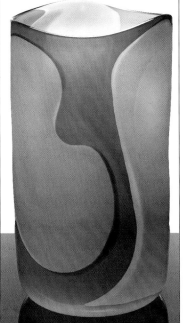

are applied to the surface, the process is known as 'overlay'. Techniques pioneered by the Scandinavian industry during the early twentieth century have been adopted with enthusiasm. The 'Graal' technique involves a glass form being developed on the blowing iron. This is cooled and worked cold by methods such as cutting and sandblasting, before being re-heated and finished with further clear or coloured overlays. Sophisticated decoration can be integrated into the blown glass. A further refinement of the technique, called 'Ariel', produces air bubbles in the glass formed into intricate and often intriguing patterns.

'By the Sea', a Graal glass cylinder by Annica Sandström and David Kaplan (Lindean Mill Glass), 1997.

'Reflection Blue/Ruby' by June Kingsbury, using blown glass with Graal technique.

Right: 'Carousel Collection' by Anthony Stern, 1999. Using a Victorian 'pineapple mould', Stern achieves an air-inclusion technique similar to Ariel.

Mould blowing is a major technique that has been used by industrial glass-makers for thousands of years. Although it is used by some studio glass-makers as one of their approaches, its use is still fairly uncommon in the studio context.

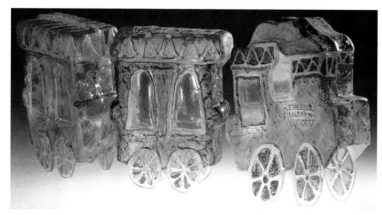

A mould-blown glass form by Paula Andrews, 1988.

17

'Sister Marie' by Liz Lowe, 1998. Using a variety of techniques of mould blowing (into a soft-sand mould) and decorating by enamelling, lustre decoration and engraving, Lowe works collaboratively with her partner, John Cook.

Casting and kiln working

From the late 1970s there has been something of a move away from glass-blowing as the dominant approach to studio glass-making in Britain. As well as the difficulty and expense of setting up a blowing workshop, the crafts skills required by glass-blowing take many years to achieve. Studio glass-blowers can find themselves in competition with manufacturers who reproduce glass vessel forms more quickly, cheaply and consistently.

There has also been a reaction to the early emphasis on the immediacy and self-expression of free blowing. Many now use techniques allowing greater control over the making process and the outcome. The pioneering work in the casting of glass being carried out in other parts of Europe has been very influential. This includes the work of Bertil Vallien in Sweden, using sand-casting techniques, and the strong glass-making community found in the Czech Republic, which has a long tradition of fine glass-making that survived the downfall of Communism.

A bowl, sand-cast by Amanda Brisbane, 2001.

18

Above left: A sand-cast form, *c.*1975, by John Cook, comprising found objects and 'concerning women, ancient fertility figures, angels and dreams'.

Above right: 'Bamboo Scroll' by Colin Reid, 1999. A commission for Shanghai Library, China.

Approaches to casting fall into two main categories. The first, 'free' casting, is similar to the processes of the metal foundry. Molten glass (also known as 'metal') is poured into a mould made of a material such as compressed sand. This allows a free approach to form, as the models for the finished piece can either be made by the glass-maker beforehand in a material such as plaster, or 'found' objects can be used. Casting can produce very robust glass objects and the process lends itself to sculptural uses. Cast glass is now the main vehicle by which this otherwise fragile material is used in a public art context.

The other main category is kiln casting. This depends on accurate control of the kiln environment. In terms of philosophy and approach, kiln casting is very different to glass-blowing. The process takes place over time and away from the eyes of the maker. The mould is usually made from a composition based on plaster of Paris, while the model is often made out of wax. Factors such as the size of the glass pieces used, the placing of pieces of coloured glass in the

Left: Plaster moulds being made by David Reekie from modelled-wax originals.

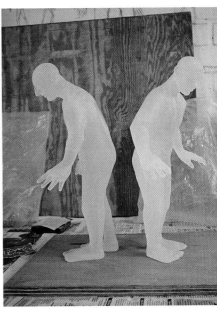

Above left: Moulds of David Reekie's figures set up in the kiln. The spaces above the mould are reservoirs that hold the raw glass cullet. This melts into the mould in the heat of the kiln.

Above right: Completed glass figures by David Reekie.

Right: Fired glass and copper-powder vessels by Maggie Hilton, who said: 'I build materials such as copper wire and powder and metal foils into my glass pieces, the result being highly textured, sometimes eroded surfaces.'

Three wax models with copper-wire decoration awaiting the making of the mould. By Maggie Hilton.

A mould for one of Tlws Johnson's pieces, filled with recycled glass ready for firing.

Right: 'Triad', a *pâte de verre* vessel by Ros Conway, 1997. Originally trained as a jeweller, Conway has used the *pâte de verre* process to explore forms that reveal an affinity with the sea.

reservoir above the mould, and the firing temperatures (usually in the range 800°C [1472°F] to 1000°C [1832°F]) can have a decisive influence on the final outcome. As with free casting, extensive cold finishing is used to bring out the internal qualities of the piece.

The *pâte de verre* process has been invented and reinvented by glass-makers since ancient times. It is one of the most significant types of kiln process used by British studio glass-makers. It involves a crushed-glass paste bound with water and a medium such as gum arabic being pressed into a mould and then fired. Temperature control is crucial, as the aim is to fuse the paste without letting it become molten. The final piece retains the granularity of the original paste and can produce some very delicate and beautiful effects. A range of types of *pâte de verre* is possible, often depending on the coarseness or smoothness of the original paste.

Right: 'Nereid 2', a *pâte de verre* vessel by Ros Conway, 1997.

'Progressive Series No. 6', a vessel form in *pâte de verre* and perforated copper sheet by Diana Hobson, 1986.

21

'No. 185', a laminated glass bowl with metal, by Sara McDonald, who said: 'I hope my use of colour, design, material and form are successful in creating objects of a quietly enduring quality, for that has always been my intention.'

Below: Glass tableware in Japanese style, made by Neil McCutcheon using the slumping technique.

Kiln forming techniques depend on glass elements, such as sheet glass, deforming consistently under the heat of the kiln in a variety of ways. These techniques include fusing, where different elements of glass are bonded by the heat, and glass lamination, in which layers of different-coloured glass, and occasionally other materials such as metal foils, are made up. Techniques such

Above: Fiona Houghton-Parker preparing flat-glass blanks before heating them in the kiln.

The flat glass slumps when heated in the kiln into plaster of Paris moulds.

22

Sean Hunter's modern lampworking bench and torch.

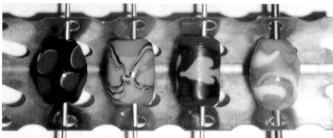

Glass beads designed by Sean Hunter using lampworking techniques.

as 'sagging' and 'slumping' also rely on deformation, usually into or over a shaped mould. Slumping is the process by which the glass element is deformed but retains its original thickness. Sagging is more extreme and can result in final shapes that are very different from the original glass element.

Lampworking

'Warm' glass techniques, generally characterised under the term 'lampworking', comprise a variety of approaches. Lampworking can be carried out with little of the expensive equipment required by other processes. It is therefore an accessible type of glass-making, forming a bridge between the amateur and the professional. Many will know the technique from the 'end of the pier' studios producing decorative items such as glass animals. Studio glass-makers have taken this process and used it as a starting point for pieces that are then finished at the furnace. The basic oil or gas lamp of the nineteenth century has been left behind and replaced by sophisticated gas torches capable of a high heat and able to melt and work with a wide range of glass.

The most extreme form of lampworking is with neon. Neon lighting is usually associated with advertising displays. However, since the early 1980s, studio glass-makers have broken away from the standardised forms used for commercially produced neon signs. Lampworking techniques have been utilised to produce abstract,

Above left: William Manson Snr making lampwork 'Lupins' as part of the process of producing handmade tableweights (1997).

Above right: 'Red Toots', 1996, by Peter Freeman, the leading British neon artist.

'Brambles' (left) and 'Strawberry' (right) paperweights, produced using the lampwork process by William Manson Jnr, 2000.

asymmetrical shapes with the possibilities of neon pushed to the extreme. Neon can be used for individual, artistic outcomes as well as commercial displays.

Coldworking techniques

Techniques used on the cold glass object are almost as diverse as those involving heat and have been in existence for as long. Studio glass-makers use basically the same cold decorating techniques as

Deborah Fladgate
polishing the 'portholes'
on one of her boat forms.

Left: 'Reed Boat, blue (KY16)' (1997) by Deborah Fladgate, who said: 'The Reed Boat involves extensive cutting and allows an exploration into the depths of glass letting light into the walls.'

industrial centres such as Stourbridge in the West Midlands, but to very different effect. It is sadly ironic that studio work has flourished while the industry that brought so many of these processes to the fore has diminished so dramatically.

Coldworking that involves deep invasion of the glass surface makes use of highly refractive glass, such as lead 'crystal' containing 25 per cent or more lead by content. This produces glass that is soft and workable but also sparkles when cut.

The deepest and most radical method of cutting or carving into the glass body (which has been blown or moulded first) involves rapidly spinning wheels made of either carborundum or diamond composite being applied to the surface of the glass object. Deep cuts are also made using sandblasting methods, which involve a gun firing an abrasive mixed with compressed air at an object enclosed within a booth. Surface effects can be varied by using different grades of abrasive and by altering the length of exposure to the sandblast. Sandblasting involves carefully masking areas of the object from the abrasive with resistant substances such as plastic and rubber using stencils designed and made beforehand.

Associated with wheel cutting is copperwheel engraving. This skilled technique applies the object to a rapidly spinning wheel, which is lubricated by oil that also contains the abrasive. Studio makers still use the traditional approach, where the glass object is

Above: Slumped bowls with sandblasted decoration by Fiona Houghton-Parker, 1996.

Left: Fiona Houghton-Parker working at a sandblasting machine, 1999.

applied to the fixed copper wheel, but this involves a high degree of dexterity. Towards the end of the twentieth century the 'flexidrive' became popular, using technology similar to the old-fashioned dental drill. The spinning head can be freely moved and is applied to the surface of the glass object. The most basic cutting and engraving technique is that of diamond-point or stipple engraving.

Below left: Katharine Coleman engraving 'Forest Fire' at a static copper wheel, 1996.

Below right: 'Forest Fire' by Katharine Coleman, 1996. Green over an orange overlay, with the front face ground and polished by hand to reveal animals fleeing from and into the flames as the forest burns.

'Noah II' by Peter Dreiser, 1989, engraved by drill and wheel. Dreiser, who trained in Germany, uses his mastery of traditional techniques to achieve an easy, free-flowing style.

A simple hand-held stylus tool with a diamond tip is used to scratch or engrave the surface of the glass. It is often associated in the British context with the pioneering work of Laurence Whistler.

Alongside these mechanical approaches to decoration is a range of chemical treatments. Acid etching produces similar effects to cutting

'Only Rock and Roll' by David Prytherch, 1993. Prytherch uses flexible drive equipment to carve and engrave his pieces.

Above: 'Tricolour Bowl' by Morag Gordon, who said: 'For me a bowl is almost sharing or containing. A personal response to life and how we act and interact with each other – reaching out to each other, touching, not touching.'

Left: Morag Gordon acid-etching.

and engraving, using strong solutions of hydrofluoric and sulphuric acid that attack the surface of the glass. Acid etching, like sandblasting, relies on careful masking of the glass surface and accurate timing of the period of acid immersion in order to produce decorative effects. The obvious health dangers mean that elaborate protective equipment and clothing have to be used. Many studio glass-makers use commercially produced acid etching pastes that are easier to control and are less harmful to health.

Enamelling is a common method of applying colour to an object. In its traditional form, enamel is a soft glass with a low melting temperature that contains metallic oxides that provide the colouring ingredient. It can come in a water-based or oil-based medium and can be either painted on to the surface of the glass prior to firing or applied using various techniques such as transfers and screen printing. Enamel colours can be very susceptible to even slight changes in the kiln atmosphere. 'Cold' enamels, which do not require firing and which make use of resins, have been gaining popularity alongside other materials such as acrylic paints. They are less robust than 'hot' enamels, however. For this reason, they are often associated with decorative rather than utilitarian items.

From craft towards art

The diverse nature of studio glass-making is probably unique within British crafts, and this tends to make categorisation difficult. One way of understanding much of the activity is to recognise the influence of early hot-glass courses. The work of Sam Herman at the Royal College of Art, for instance, provided the combination of technical support and artistic freedom needed to nurture many glass-makers who are now leading figures. Dillon Clarke, one of his earliest students, described his influence (1976) as 'his feeling for colour, his ability to create rich swirling colours, emphasising the fluid quality of the molten glass'.

Herman's students included Ray Flavell, now Head of Glass and Architectural Glass at Edinburgh College of Art, John Cook, who was Head of Ceramics and Glass at De Montfort University, Leicester, and Pauline Solven. Flavell's work moved fairly rapidly away from the freedom espoused by Herman towards the control of technique he learned subsequently at the Orrefors Glass School in Sweden. This has been put to the use of art (his work is represented in most of the major national museum collections) and design, with consultancy work for industrial glass firms such as Stevens & Williams and Royal Brierley Crystal. John Cook also has created a balance between artistic freedom and design. His surreal sand-cast pieces can be contrasted with his work as a visiting designer in the glass industries of Czechoslovakia and Venice during the 1960s and 1970s.

'Form 5' by Sam Herman in free-blown coloured glass.

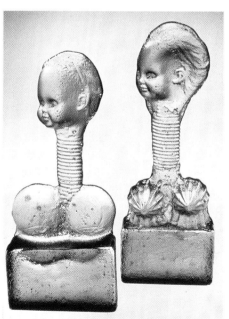

Cast pieces by John Cook, 1977. They were featured in *Life* magazine in 1979.

Objects made by one of the most experienced Venetian glass-makers, Mario Colleli, from designs by John Cook, 1970.

By comparison, Pauline Solven has remained closer to Herman's original ethos. She is an unusual example of a glass-blower who has mastered the difficulties of working alone with the process. She produces pieces that emphasise the painterly use of colour, saying that 'before approaching the furnace, I create an intricate arrangement of glass colours in powder and canes on a steel table. During the making process, I transfer this to the clear glass on the blow iron, and add further detail as I work. The piece is finished with sandblasting and acid etching.'

The Royal College course was, in Britain, unique in offering a postgraduate opportunity for the study of glass. Makers who had studied other media at undergraduate level could transfer their interests and experience to glass. This was the situation during the

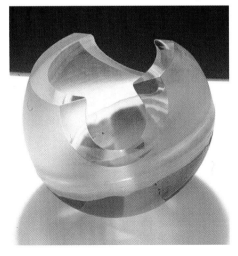

'Rocking Globe: Sail d'Azure' by Pauline Solven, 1985.

Above: 'Paintwork IV' by Pauline Solven, 2000.

Right: 'Staggered Stack' by Pauline Solven, 1993. This series was inspired by the qualities of Pisan architecture.

1970s with several students, who are now leaders in the field. Annette Meech was originally a student of ceramics, as was Diana Hobson, while Anthony Stern left a successful career in the film industry to take up glass-making.

Diana Hobson was seeking an extension to her experiments with enamelling techniques when she alighted upon *pâte de verre*. It was a process that summed up the fragility and translucency of glass for her. Her triumph has been to retain these qualities in the material

Right: 'New Texture Series No. 1' by Diana Hobson, 1987. This piece demonstrates Hobson's unique approach to the *pâte de verre* process, integrating the material with beach sand, crushed red brick, small stones and metal mesh.

Below: 'Multi Coloured Form', Diana Hobson's first successful vessel in the *pâte de verre* process, 1983.

31

'Fragment of a Circle' by Diana Hobson in stone, bronze and *pâte de verre*, 1994.

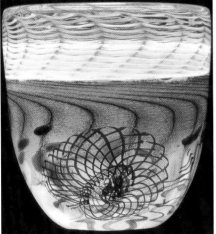

while at the same time integrating found materials into it. Hobson has gradually moved away from vessels towards the more overtly sculptural. This has also resulted in a move away from *pâte de verre*.

Pâte de verre is a technique that takes a long time to master. Its practitioners tend to become specialists in the material. By contrast, Anthony Stern has used a wide variety of techniques to produce objects ranging from series production through to individual artistic statements. The series pieces frequently pay homage to ancient

Left: 'Long Beach' by Anthony Stern, 1996.

Below: 'Sky Panel' by Anthony Stern, late 1990s. This panel was made using traditional 'cylinder glass' methods.

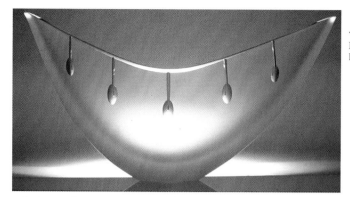

'Boat with Dangling
Fenders (KY96)' by
Deborah Fladgate, 2000.

techniques that are interpreted for the modern consumer, and to the
influence of foreign, particularly tribal, cultures. Stern's individual
pieces reflect his first career as a photographer and film-maker. His
seascape vessels and plaques, for instance, are 'essentially
"transparencies" which come to life by the action of transmitted
light. In nature there is fluid movement between the sea, sky and
rock and I aim to capture moments of this process.'

While Stern's work demonstrates a free and expressive attitude to
the medium, Deborah Fladgate's approach to glass has evolved
through periods of assistantship to both Stern and Pauline Solven
towards creating tightly controlled glass objects. Her series of boat-
shaped forms involves extensive coldworking and finishing, and the
emphasis on variations of a single form has brought what she has
described as a 'more acute focus' to her work.

The diverse output from graduates of the Royal College during the
1980s and 1990s reflects their willingness to be adventurous and
experimental. In this context, the work of Anna Dickinson deserves
special mention. Her trademark technique is electroforming, a

'Aurelia', a chandelier in
crystal and stainless steel
by Neil Wilkin, 2000. With
a diameter of 3 metres, this
is a demonstration of
Wilkin's skill as a glass-
maker. He has worked co-
operatively with a number
of makers, including
Pauline Solven, Anna
Dickinson and Rachel
Woodman, as well as
designing for Dartington
Crystal Ltd.

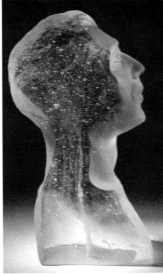

Far left: An electroformed glass vase by Anna Dickinson, 1999.

Left: 'Perceptions of Reality III' by Bruno Romanelli, 1996, made by the lost-wax casting process. Romanelli said: 'The piece represents my view of us as human beings. The surface being calm, revealing little of the internal chaos that obviously goes on within all of us.'

'Twisted Plate' by Jane Beebe, late 1990s. She said: 'My work is concerned with the creation of movement through line and form. I enjoy pushing the vessel to the limits: is it a functional item or is it sculpture?'

laborious process involving building up metallic layers on the surface of the glass and often taking weeks to complete. Objects relate closely to her travelling experiences, and particularly to the artistic traditions of tribal Africa. Jane Beebe's career is that of a glass-maker whose work ranges from explorations of the interface between function and art through to one-off and series commissions for both industry and individual clients.

The work of those who graduated from the Royal College in the 1990s represents steps towards the resolution of an issue that has concerned studio glass-makers since the 1960s: namely, the place of glass-making on the axis between art and craft. As one answer, Bruno Romanelli and Emma Woffenden produce work that is uncompromisingly sculptural in its emphasis. Woffenden's work makes use of the mould-blowing technique to produce mysterious, darkly coloured abstract pieces, while Romanelli employs the lost-wax casting process to produce figurative sculpture that investigates the nature of the human condition.

'Tearseed' by Angela Thwaites, 1998. A graduate of West Surrey College of Art and Design, Thwaites uses the casting process and extensive cold finishing to develop sculptural themes relating to parts of the body, such as the eyes.

Left: 'Stem' by Keith Cummings, 1997. Lost-wax cast glass with metal inclusions.

The role of other educational centres as a focus for glass-making activity should not be underestimated. These include courses at the Stourbridge College of Art, the West Surrey College of Art and Design, Farnham, and the Universities of Sunderland and Staffordshire.

Of these, the Stourbridge College of Art (now part of Wolverhampton University) stands out for its role in promoting kiln-forming techniques. The significance of Stourbridge has largely been a result of the teaching activities of Professor Keith Cummings, whose interest in glass-making stems from a background in the fine arts that predates the arrival of studio glass-making in Britain. The lost-wax cast pieces that he produces are small in scale and yet intricate in their weaving together of glass with wire, bronze and fabricated metals in a process that can

'Wedge' by Keith Cummings, 1998. Cast glass and bronze.

'Gemfruit' by Keith Cummings, 2000. Lost-wax cast glass with metal inclusions.

take many months to complete. Cummings's technical skill has been disseminated over the years via his seminal book *Techniques of Glass Forming* (1980) and through the students he has taught since 1968 at Stourbridge, many of whom are now leading practitioners. Of these, Brian Blanthorn, Tessa Clegg, David Reekie and Colin Reid are all outstanding in having extended kiln-forming processes in various ways.

The work of Brian and Jenny Blanthorn extends fusing and slumping techniques to bring out the full refractive possibilities of the glass, for example with a range of opalescent 'pebble' forms. Each piece is painstakingly cut, polished and re-fired to achieve the end result. Brian Blanthorn's career-long interest in the power of line, originating from a fascination with the qualities of geological strata, has resulted in shapes that include the utilitarian, the decorative and the sculptural.

Colin Reid's work with lost-wax casting techniques also represents a journey, this time from the utilitarian form to the sculptural, and indeed towards public art in his later pieces. Like

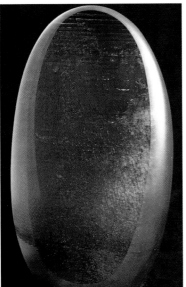

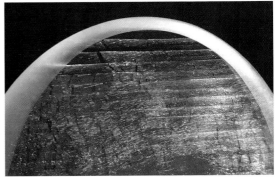

Left: 'W233', a multi-laminated pebble form by Brian and Jenny Blanthorn, 2001.

Below: 'W233', a detail of the multi-laminated pebble form by Brian and Jenny Blanthorn, 2001.

Above: A bowl in turquoise with copper-black block-printed ground by Brian and Jenny Blanthorn, 1990.
Below: An opalescent bowl with complex block-printed pattern by Brian and Jenny Blanthorn, 1990.

Right: 'R1000' by Colin Reid in kiln-cast glass, 2001.

Below: 'Flacon' by Colin Reid in lost-wax cast glass, 1985. Reid says: 'This group of perfume vessels from the 1980s reflected an interest in abstracting the vessel form. To work as flacons they must have certain elements: a hollow interior and stopper. However, the function need not dictate form, which is quite sculptural.'

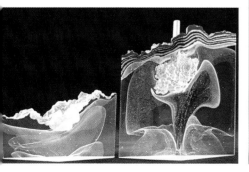

'River Rocks' by Colin Reid, 2000. A commission for the River Lune Millennium Park.

Brian Blanthorn's, they are completed via a long process of sandblasting, grinding and polishing in order to bring out the interior qualities of the glass. Crucially, though, he is concerned to avoid too great a reliance on the innate 'prettiness' of the material. He says that 'The piece must work as a form in a bland material like plaster and not rely on the beauty and the magic of glass to enhance it and make it work.' Reid develops his forms by making use of found objects that form the basis of the moulds and are sometimes also integrated into the finished piece.

David Reekie also uses lost-wax casting techniques to create figurative sculptures that operate simultaneously on a number of levels. The obvious humour within them conceals often biting social commentary, leading his work to be discussed as 'Hogarthian'. References range from frustration at the policies of the Thatcher governments to concerns with the dangers of cloning. Reekie's work communicates the absurdities and frustrations of the human condition so well that they have won him international acclaim and a dedicated following on both sides of the Atlantic.

The work of Tessa Clegg and Gayle Matthias has taken kiln processes in different directions. Clegg's work from the late 1990s has developed dramatically away from pleated bowl forms (originally developed from a paper-folding exercise) towards far more overtly sculptural work. Made by the lost-wax process, the

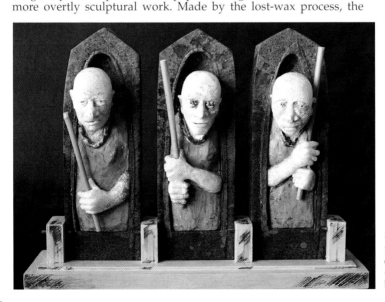

'The Lookouts' by David Reekie, 1987. Cast glass with wooden base and bamboo staves.

Right: 'Uncertain Situation III' by David Reekie, 1994. Lost-wax cast glass with enamel colour.

Below: '2001: A Human Oddity?' by David Reekie, 2001. Lost-wax cast glass, copper wire and painted wood.

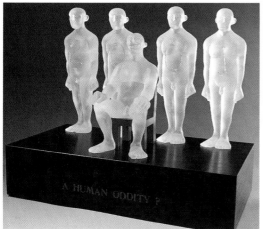

objects make a play on the nature of function and challenge the boundaries between art and design. Matthias's work is a technical *tour de force* that combines many of the kiln-forming processes within individual forms. Her 'Body Series' of sculptures, for instance, makes use of '*pâte de verre* outer shells; crushed, fused, lead crystal cellular internal structures and lost-wax cast, polished, crystal bases and centre cores'.

The fame of Stourbridge as a centre for instruction in kiln-forming techniques should not disguise the fact that many leading glass-blowers were also taught there, including Pauline Solven, Fleur Tookey and Karlin Rushbrooke. Rushbrooke has combined

'Body I', made by Gayle Matthias using a variety of kiln-formed glass techniques.

Loop-stemmed jugs by Karlin Rushbrooke, c.1976.

a thirty-year career as a glass-maker with work as a builder. His early work reflects in its humorous approach to the making of glass objects the influences of the funk art movement. Later work includes figurative decoration of the surface of the piece using sandblasting and engraving in an attempt to depict mankind 'with amusement, despair, compassion and hope'. Fleur Tookey's work is based on a career specialising in the application of colour to free-blown forms. Colour is created by the hot application of powders, chips and trails to the surface of the glass, and her finished work encompasses a wide range of vessel shapes and forms.

'Bubble Bottles' by Fleur Tookey, c.1985.

'Pebble Bowls' by Fleur Tookey, 1998.

A bowl form by Fleur Tookey, made at The Glasshouse, 1987.

Tookey, together with another graduate of Stourbridge, Catherine Hough, is representative of another phase in the development of studio glass-making in Britain. They were early members of The Glasshouse, a co-operative company set up in Covent Garden, London, in 1969 with the support of Sam Herman. Managed almost single-handedly by Pauline Solven for the first few years of its existence, The Glasshouse was the first of a series of similar organisations that provided an essential bridge between the educational world and the commercial. As well as including Solven, Tookey and Hough, The Glasshouse acted as a base and launch pad for many other important glass-makers, including Peter Layton and David Taylor.

The frontage of The Glasshouse, looking through to the showroom, soon after it opened in 1970.

Catherine Hough is best known for free-blown bottle forms. These are extensively coldworked using a variety of techniques, including grinding, polishing, cutting and texturing using diamond and carborundum wheels as well as sandblasting. For many years, Hough worked in partnership with Simon Moore, who blew the initial 'blanks' at their collaboration (together with the American maker Steven Newell) of Glassworks (London) Ltd. David Taylor, whose background was originally in jewellery design, is one of Europe's leading furnace-technology designers and manufacturers as well as a studio glass-maker. His work has similarities with that of Hough in its concern with small vessel forms, but the meticulous and exquisite perfume bottles that he produces through a process of carving and acid etching show a concern with colour and with a play on the internal qualities of the glass.

'Dancing Bottle' by Catherine Hough, 1989, who says: 'The aim was to transform this heavy solid piece of glass into a form with flowing lines and contrasting clear and opaque surfaces, which give lightness and movement.'

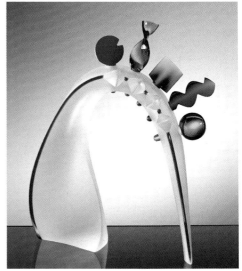

A perfume-bottle form by David Taylor, early 1990s.

The foundation of the London Glassblowing Workshop in 1970 by Peter Layton marked another stage in the development of the studio glass-making movement in Britain. Since its inception, many glass-makers have passed through the organisation, including Norman Stuart Clarke and, later, Max Lamb and David Flower. It is now the oldest glass-blowing studio in the United Kingdom. Layton's work consists of free-blown pieces that are intended to be unique. They are highly coloured and intricately decorated, drawing in subject matter from Layton's interests in beachcombing and from the qualities of ice and snow. Alongside this vessel-oriented output, Peter Layton Associates was established in 1993 to produce large-scale, one-off pieces to commissions from a diverse range of clients including architects and cruise lines.

Glass engravers have tended to be regarded as something of a separate community within the studio glass-making movement. They have their own professional societies, and the relatively few educational opportunities available mean that they are often self-taught or have come into contact with influential figures such as Helen Munro Turner at the Edinburgh College of Art. Moreover, the relatively low cost of setting up a glass-engraving studio, and the emphasis on technical skill and painstaking, time-consuming work, mean that glass engravers usually work on their own. The tradition of glass engraving in Britain is a long one, but its utilisation for studio glassworking is rather more modern and can be seen to have its roots in the work of engravers such as John Hutton, the *émigré* engraver from New Zealand, and the diamond-point engraver Laurence Whistler.

Below left: 'Jackson Pollock Pot', a blown form by Norman Stuart Clarke, 1989.

Below right: 'Tahiti Bowl' by Norman Stuart Clarke, 1992, in free-blown iridised glass.

'Market Day, Hereford' by Ronald Pennell in Rock Crystal and reverse-wheel engraved, 1968.

Outstanding work is being done by contemporary glass engravers who include Professor Ronald Pennell, Alison Kinnaird, Katharine Coleman, Peter Dreiser and David Prytherch. Pennell is a maker with an international reputation for his ingenious and humorous engraved scenes based on reactions to life's vagaries and to the countryside and culture of Herefordshire, where he has lived since 1964. He came to glass engraving almost accidentally, having already established himself as an artist in bronze and in the natural glass known as Rock Crystal. Alison Kinnaird MBE is similarly well known. Trained by Harold Gordon and by Helen Munro Turner at the Edinburgh

Above: 'Pulling Together' by Ronald Pennell in green and brown over-cased glass with wheel-engraved intaglio, Graal technique, 1997.

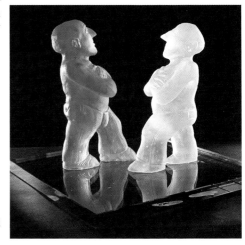

'Toe to Toe' by Ronald Pennell in cast and carved glass on cut base, 1999.

44

'Eostra', wheel-engraved by Alison Kinnaird, 1989.

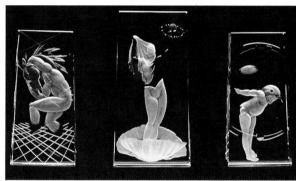

'Triptych' by Alison Kinnaird, 1994.

College of Art, her figurative work, which makes use of optical crystal, attempts to draw on the innate qualities of glass while also telling a story: 'Its purity and clarity can give an otherworldliness to the images that it holds, its transparency can be a metaphor for insight on the human soul.'

The National Glass Centre, Sunderland, is purpose-built to explore modern glass-making in one of Britain's most significant industrial glass-making areas.

Further reading

Beard, G. *International Modern Glass*. Barrie & Jenkins, 1976.
Bray, C. *Dictionary of Glass*. A. & C. Black, 1995.
Cummings, K. *The Techniques of Kiln-Formed Glass*. A. & C. Black, 1997.
Flavell, R., and Smale, C. *Studio Glassmaking*. Van Nostrand Reinhold, 1974.
Frantz, S.K. *Contemporary Glass*. Harry N. Abrams, 1989.
Klein, D. *Glass: A Contemporary Art*. Collins, 1989.
Layton, P. *Glass Art*. A. & C. Black, 1996.
Littleton, H. *Glassblowing: A Search for Form*. Van Nostrand Reinhold, 1971.
Peace, D. *Glass Engraving: Lettering and Design*. Batsford, 1985.
Ricke, H. *New Glass in Europe*. Verlagsanstalt Handwerk, 1990.
Stern, R. *Let There Be Neon*. Academy Editions, 1980.
Tait, H. *Five Thousand Years of Glass*. British Museum Press, 1991.
Vaudour, C. *The Art of Contemporary Glass*. Armand Colin, 1993.
Yelle, R.W. *Glass Art: From Urban Glass*. Schiffer Publishing, 2000.

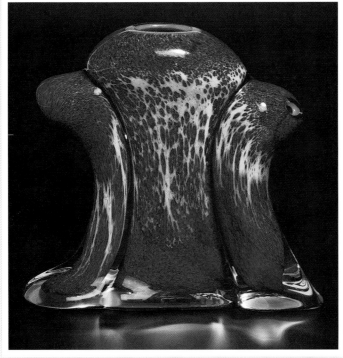

'Lazuli Trio Vase', blown by Peter Layton, 2001.

Places to visit

Broadfield House Glass Museum, Compton Drive, Kingswinford, West Midlands DY6 9NS. Telephone: 01384 812745.

Castle Museum, Castle Road, Nottingham NG1 6EL. Telephone: 0115 915 3651.

The Cowdy Gallery, 31 Culver Street, Newent, Gloucestershire GL18 1DB. Telephone: 01531 821173.

The Crafts Council, 44a Pentonville Road, London N1 9BY. Telephone: 020 7278 7700. Website: www.craftscouncil.org.uk

Dartington Crystal, School Lane, Torrington, Devon EX38 7AN. Telephone: 01805 626262. Website: www.dartington.co.uk

Fitzwilliam Museum, Trumpington Street, Cambridge CB2 1RB. Telephone: 01223 332900. Website: www.fitzmuseum.cam.ac.uk

Glasgow Art Gallery and Museum, Kelvingrove, Glasgow G3 1AG. Telephone: 0141 287 2699.

Museum Ulster, Botanic Gardens, Belfast BT9 5AB. Telephone: 028 9038 3000. Website: www.ulstermuseum.org.uk

National Glass Centre, Liberty Way, Sunderland SR6 0GL. Telephone: 0191 515 5555. Website: www.info@nationalglasscentre.com

Shipley Art Gallery, Prince Consort Road, Gateshead, Tyne and Wear NE8 4JB. Telephone: 0191 477 1495.

Victoria and Albert Museum, Cromwell Road, South Kensington, London SW7 2RL. Telephone: 020 7942 2000. Website: www.vam.ac.uk

World of Glass, Chalon Way East, St Helens, Merseyside WA10 1BX. Telephone: 01744 22766. Website: www.info@worldofglass.com

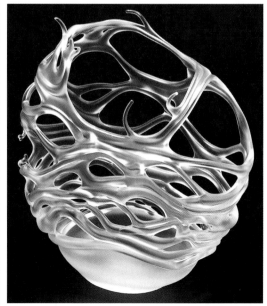

A blown 'Ice Basket' form by Peter Layton, 2001.

Index